Relaxing T

A revolutionary ap

Dan Jones

Connect with Dan Jones:

www.DanJonesHypnosis.com

First Edition 2016

Published by Dan Jones

Copyright © Daniel Jones 2016

Daniel Jones asserts the moral right to be identified as the author of this work.

All rights reserved. No part of this publication may be reproduced, stored in a retrieval system, or transmitted, in any form or by any means, electronic, mechanical, photocopying, recording, or otherwise, without the prior written permission of the publishers or author.

ISBN 978-1539976882

In loving memory of

Reg Searle

Always in the mood for a sentimental journey

Cycling through time

Counting on us to follow along

To each and every line

Contents

Introduction	7
Relaxing Children's Tales	11
Mystery of the Yellow Lake	15
Timmy's Tall Tale	21
The Secret Garden	29
Saving Prince Charming	35
Jonny's Rotten Apple	43
The Curious Discovery	49
The Butterfly and the Bee	55
The Clown Who Never Grew Up	61
The Early Worm Catches the Bird	71
Patches in the Dog House	79
Milton's Magical Mystery Tour	85

Introduction

I have been working with children, teens and parents for over 15 years. The main areas I have focused on have been problems with sleep, and behaviour more generally, including child/teen-to-parent domestic abuse and violence. One of the most important things I teach to parents and children is how to relax. When I teach family courses, I always start each parents' session with a guided meditation and relaxing breathing technique; the children also have a guided meditation and - depending on their age, understanding and engagement - I like to teach them a relaxing breathing technique too, breathing in counting to seven, and out counting to ten. The longer in-breath triggers the relaxation response.

To keep children involved in the relaxation experience, I have always found, especially with younger children, that a guided story works better than guiding a child through a guided experience or meditation that perhaps seems more "adult".

Children can be very active, and this is good. But at the same time, children need to learn to be still, calm and relaxed. That is where this book comes in. It offers a different way to tell stories to children.

My previous children's story book, *Sleepy Bedtime Tales*, was a collection of stories for parents and carers to read to their children to help them to fall asleep. The stories in that book were based around my approach to helping children fall asleep. This book is similar, in that it uses many of the same techniques as in the previous book, but instead of focusing on helping children to fall asleep, the stories in this book are to help children to relax. (That being said, children may still relax to the point that they fall asleep if they are tired.)

Like the previous book, the stories in this book are written to be read to four- to seven-year-olds; they will work with younger children, and with older children, too, but younger children will be less likely to understand the stories, and older children may find them too simple. The stories in this book all contain the same main characters as the stories in *Sleepy Bedtime Tales*; they are just on different adventures.

The stories in this book can be read to groups of children, or to individual children; the book can be used in primary schools, nurseries, and playgroups at story-time. There is growing evidence that children learning mindfulness meditation are calmer, more emotionally resilient, and better able to handle stress.

The approach used in this book is based on mindfulness and meditation. The stories are like guided meditations for children, with a structure to follow. As the children listen to the stories, they are learning to relax and are developing the skills they need in order to be able to manage stress and increase their emotional resilience.

Learning happens by recognising patterns and applying them to different situations. Throughout history, this has been how children have learnt important lessons from elders, especially prior to written texts. Children would be taught stories, within which were many patterns about how to behave in different situations. An example of this would be Homer's *Iliad* and *Odyssey*.

One skill children learn as they grow up is how to use metaphors. Some children struggle with consciously understanding metaphors, like children with autism - they can take longer to begin to understand them as having an alternative meaning, but the patterns being presented still become embedded in the mind of the child.

The stories in this book are all based around helping children to relax. The techniques used to achieve this are rapport-building skills, which many people will recognise as things that they do and use already, but they may not necessarily use them in quite this way. So when a parent is trying to relax a child, he/she will change tone of voice, perhaps talking softly, slowly and rhythmically. Unfortunately, stories aren't usually written around this way of speaking; the stories in this book, however, are specifically written with how they will be read firmly in mind.

When trying to calm or relax children, parents also say relevant words with calming or relaxing emphasis. Most children's stories aren't written with key words or phrases in them that parents can say. Again, though, this book has key words and phrases marked out in *italics* for the reader to emphasise. It doesn't take too many emphasised words for people to pick up on the ideas conveyed by those words. These stories have intentionally been written to sound as much like ordinary stories as possible.

Relaxing Children's Tales

Most of these stories should take between seven and ten minutes to read. *The Clown Who Never Grew Up* is the exception, at about 13 minutes long. They are written to be read slowly and calmly. Start by suggesting that your child sits or lies down comfortably and closes their eyes while you read to them. If you are reading to a group of children, you could ask them to sit or lie down on mats on the floor. It doesn't really matter how the children sit or lie, as long as they are comfortable. It is often preferable that they don't have legs crossed, because this can sometimes be uncomfortable.

Children have a tendency to move around and fidget. This is alright. It doesn't matter if they fidget, or if they open their eyes. I usually just suggest something like "that's right, you can take a moment to get more comfortable". Likewise, if you catch them opening their eyes, I might suggest something like "that's it, and you can let your eyes close again as you drift back to the story".

When I have read stories like these with groups of children, especially slightly older children who perhaps aren't familiar with each other, some of the children usually open their eyes to look around and see if everyone is doing the same. Usually, just carrying on confidently without being fazed by this is the best option. The children often just close their eyes again and carry on with the experience.

I have held groups with teens who are on the course due to their violent and aggressive behaviour in the home. They can sometimes be self-conscious about closing their eyes and relaxing in a group of five to eleven other teens with similar issues and group facilitators, and yet even they follow along and engage well. They will often laugh, and mess around a little initially, and will open their eyes, but because the person reading the meditative story just carries on reading calmly, they tend to close their eyes and join in. Meditative stories are one of the most popular elements of the courses, for adults and children of all ages.

As you read the stories, it is good to read in time with when your child breathes out. If they are breathing too fast, you can read in time with two, or even three breaths. Pause briefly as your child breathes in, and then read as they breathe out. If, for example, you are reading across three breaths then you would: read as they breathe out, still be reading as they breathe in, then still be reading as they breathe out and in again, before finishing the sentence you are reading as they breathe out. Then, pause as they breathe in, before then repeating the same as above for the next cycle of three breaths. You may want to pause for more than one breath in - perhaps for a breath in, a breath out, and a breath in again - before reading again.

When you finish reading a story, you can end by saying 'the end' and then suggesting the child or children can gently open their eyes after a few moments. Alternatively, you can finish reading the story where it ends, pause for a few moments, either for a minute or so, or until you see the children beginning to move, and then you can suggest that they can gently open their eyes when they are ready.

Because these stories are about relaxation, the best option is to pause briefly after you finish reading the story, and before you suggest the child can open their eyes. Ideally this pause will be as long as it takes for the child, or children to look like they are beginning to come back to the room. They are likely to start fidgeting a little more. This pause could be anywhere between 30 seconds and a couple of minutes. Generally, the longer you can make this pause the more relaxed children will be when they open their eyes.

If you are reading these stories at bedtime, or to help your child to fall asleep, you can replace the final 'eyes opening' sentence after a minute or two with the suggestion that they can drift comfortably asleep.

Mystery of the Yellow Lake

As *you close your eyes*, I'm going to tell you the story about Malcolm the rabbit and the mystery of the yellow lake, and with *your eyes closed*, you can listen to me reading this story. While I read this story, you can *begin to feel relaxed*. And as I read, you can *imagine this story* in your mind.

Malcolm the rabbit lived in the magician's hat. The world inside the hat was strange; the sky was pink and the trees grew upside-down.

One day, Malcolm hopped along to a nearby park. He followed a winding path that weaved through the upside-down trees to a lake in the centre of the park. When Malcolm reached the lake, he saw a curious sight. Usually, the water was green, but today, it was bright yellow. Malcolm could see a hedgehog sitting by the lake, crying.

He hopped over to the hedgehog "Are you okay?" Malcom asked.

"Somebody has stolen the colour blue from the lake, so the water is yellow," sobbed the hedgehog. "Please can you help me find the colour blue?"

Malcolm loved a mystery, so he told the hedgehog he would be happy to help. What Malcolm didn't know was where he would start. "Do you have any clues or ideas about who may have stolen the colour blue?" Malcolm asked the hedgehog.

"I saw a trail of blue puddles leading away from the lake... I'll show you." With that, the hedgehog led Malcolm around the lake to the blue puddles.

"How curious," Malcolm thought as he looked at the puddles, thinking about where they might lead.

Malcolm followed the blue puddles along a path leading out of the park. The puddles were quite close together; this seemed to be a sign that the thief was carrying the colour blue on foot. He wondered who might have taken the colour, and why.

After leaving the park, Malcolm continued to follow the puddles *down* the road. Malcolm felt like he had been hopping along for ages, when the puddles suddenly changed direction and led into a hole in the ground.

Malcolm got out a torch, turned it on, and hopped into the hole. The hole was wide with muddy sides. The torchlight reflected off the puddles as Malcolm continued to follow them *deeper and deeper* into the hole.

The *deeper* Malcolm hopped down the hole, the quieter it became around him, as the noises from outside the hole disappeared into the distance. Malcolm found the quiet *relaxing*. All he could hear was his feet as he bounced along.

After fifty hops, Malcolm stopped. He thought he could hear a noise coming from further down the tunnel. He needed to focus so that he could hear better. He closed his eyes and breathed in. Then, as he breathed out, he imagined a warm light shining on his head, his neck and his shoulders. He imagined this warm light *relaxing his muscles* and helping him to *focus* better on what he could hear. Then, he breathed in again, and when he breathed out, he imagined that warm *relaxing* light moving through his body - from his head down to his toes.

As the light reached his toes, Malcolm was able to *focus* his ears on the sound he could hear. It was the sound of footsteps. Malcolm wasn't far behind the thief. He continued quietly following.

After another fifty hops, Malcolm saw a light at the end of the tunnel. He hopped quietly towards this light, and when he reached it, he saw a young squirrel carrying a bucket of the colour blue.

The squirrel looked worried as it scampered over to an upside-down tree.

Malcolm decided to go and talk to the squirrel, so he hopped down from the tunnel and over to the tree.

"Is everything alright?" Malcolm asked.

The squirrel seemed surprised to see Malcolm, for the rabbit had done such a good job at keeping quiet while he followed the puddles.

"Something is wrong with my tree. I am trying to save it," the squirrel said.

Malcolm wondered what was wrong with the tree. The squirrel told him that the leaves on the tree used to be green but now they were going yellow and some of the leaves had fallen off. He had never seen this before. The squirrel said he went to the park to get some colour blue to try to fix the leaves.

"If I can make the tree drink the colour blue, hopefully it will make the yellow leaves green again," the squirrel said.

The squirrel had never experienced autumn before, and didn't realise that it was natural for the leaves on trees to change colour from green to yellow before falling off in time for winter.

Malcolm explained that when the sun starts getting *lower* in the sky and the weather begins to turn cold, trees prepare to save energy for the winter by drinking the nutrients from the leaves, which makes them change colour. The trees then drop the leaves because they don't need them over the winter, and in the spring, they grow new leaves to make new food from sunlight.

The squirrel was pleased to hear that his tree was going to be alright. He agreed to go with Malcolm back to the lake in order to return the colour blue.

Malcolm and the squirrel travelled together out of the hole, back up the road to the park, across the park and back to the lake. When they arrived at the lake, the squirrel poured the colour blue back into the yellow water, and with a splash and a swirl, the blue and yellow mixed together and the water gradually turned green again.

And, in your own time, you can gradually allow your eyes to open, as *you continue to feel relaxed.*

Timmy's Tall Tale

As *you close your eyes*, I'm going to tell you the story about Timmy's tall tale, and with *your eyes closed*, you can listen to me reading this story. While I read to you, you can *begin to feel relaxed*, and you can *imagine this story* in your mind.

One day, Timmy woke up with a strange feeling. He didn't know what the feeling was; all he knew was that it felt wrong. Timmy got out of bed, unable to shake the strange feeling. "What is this feeling?" Timmy asked himself curiously.

Timmy slid blue superhero slippers on his feet and walked down the stairs.

Halfway down the staircase, he saw something out of the corner of his eye reflected in the mirror on the wall in the corridor downstairs. He didn't know what it was. It looked like a secret passage to another dimension had just opened up in the cupboard under the stairs.

When Timmy reached the bottom of the stairs and looked, the door was shut and everything appeared to be normal. He wondered whether he really had seen something, or whether it was just his mind playing tricks on him.

Timmy went to the kitchen, sat at the breakfast table and in his usual noisy and messy way, he ate his breakfast.

"Mum," Timmy said, with a mouthful of cereal, "is there a secret passage under the stairs?"

"Of course not," Timmy's mum replied with a voice that made him feel stupid for asking.

Timmy thought to himself, 'What would mum know?'

After breakfast, he went out into the corridor to check out the cupboard under the stairs. He opened the door with a creak and peered inside.

It seemed to be normal. He could see the vacuum cleaner, a big bag of plastic bags, a box of Christmas decorations, and lots of boxes. If there was a secret passage, it definitely wasn't here now. Timmy went back upstairs to his room to play.

While Timmy was sat on his floor making a spaceship out of blocks, he suddenly felt the same strange sensation he had felt when he woke up. He had a strong feeling that he needed to go and check the cupboard under the stairs again, so he stood up from his bedroom floor and walked downstairs.

As Timmy was walking down the stairs, he saw the same strange image reflected in the mirror. He continued to descend, this time without taking his eyes off of the tunnel. When he reached the bottom of the stairs he walked over to the cupboard. The secret passage was still open - the passage was still there. It was real.

Timmy looked into the passage and could see another world. It looked like another planet; the ground was red and dusty like Mars, but there was some green soft-looking moss and dark blue pools of water. The sky looked slightly yellowish and there seemed to be two suns in the sky - one very large and dim, taking up most of the sky, and the other very small and bright with a wispy line of light. It looked like it was connecting the two stars.

Timmy wondered to himself whether he should walk through the passage and investigate this strange world. He feared, though: what if the passage disappeared again and he was trapped in this strange world?

Timmy couldn't help himself... He stepped through the passage, and with a whoosh, he vanished from his home and found himself on a silent alien planet.

The moss under Timmy's feet was soft and squidgy, the air was cool and had a sweet taste that filled his senses with each breath.

'This is a strange place,' Timmy thought to himself as he looked around.

Over in the distance, Timmy could see a light. It looked like there was a metal object. He decided to go and investigate. As he started to walk, he noticed he felt lighter than normal; it even felt like he was slightly taller than usual, too. He was able to leap into the air and it felt like he was flying. It was like he had superpowers.

When Timmy reached the metal object, he noticed that it was a building. He walked up to the front of the building to look for a way to get inside. As he stood in front of the building, a light turned on and shone into his face. The light was making a soft hum. Timmy had to close his eyes because the light was so bright.

With his eyes closed, he could feel the warmth from the light on his skin. He stood there with his eyes closed and felt the light move slowly down his head, then his shoulders, down to his body. As the light travelled slowly down through Timmy's body he could feel it making him relaxed. His shoulders were relaxing, his breathing was relaxing, his arms and legs were relaxing; the light continued travelling down through his body into his legs, right down to the tips of his toes.

After the light passed down through Timmy's body, everything went silent. Timmy didn't know whether he should open his eyes or not. He stood there for a while longer with his eyes closed, before gently opening them to look around.

When he did so, everything looked the same as it had before he closed his eyes, except that there was a doorway open in front of him. It looked as if it led into the building.

Timmy walked forward through the door and into the building. In front of him were stairs leading deep underground. He followed the stairs, heading towards the sound of chattering voices.

At the bottom of the stairs Timmy discovered a whole hidden underground city. There were shops, homes, a market, and tall orange aliens walking around everywhere. The aliens looked friendly, so Timmy spoke with one of them: "Where is this place? Where am I?" he asked.

"You are on the planet Cirrus B2, in the city of Pantheon," the alien replied, "I am Frank."

"Frank?" Timmy said, "That is an odd name for an alien."

"You are the alien," Frank replied.

Timmy thought about it for a moment and realised that here, in this place, he was the alien.

"Why can you speak English?" Timmy quizzed.

"Language is just a way of expressing thoughts to others. All thoughts are similar; we just give them different labels. We can communicate through thoughts and you understand those thoughts using your labels."

Timmy was a bit confused, but he felt like he just about understood what Frank was trying to say. Timmy wondered whether the feeling he'd had twice earlier in his bedroom was linked to these aliens.

"Yes," Frank replied, having read Timmy's thoughts. "We needed your help. We needed the help of someone that wouldn't be scared to travel through the passage to our world."

Frank explained that, on Earth, adults don't believe in things like children do. Adults see only the world they expect to see. Children can see things adults can't see. He explained that this alien world would disappear as the big sun got bigger, and the little sun was gradually eating the big sun, which was making dangerous beams of light sweep across the planet, harming anything on the surface. He told Timmy that the small star wasn't making any dangerous beams of light at the moment, so it was safe to be out on the surface for now, but every few days a beam sweeps across the planet.

Most of the aliens had left the planet, he said; just a few remained, and they now lived underground to avoid the beam. They were able to use the energy from the small star to make a passage through space. They communicated with Timmy so that he could take a powerful blue crystal back to Earth. That crystal would allow him to open a passage any time he wanted. Once the aliens permanently left the planet, they wouldn't have a way of opening a passage because they wouldn't be near the small sun. In spite of this, they had found a way to link two crystals that can make a passage between them, the alien recounted. One crystal would be kept on their new home, and the other was to be kept on Earth. This would allow the aliens to continue to visit Earth after they left their home planet.

Timmy liked the idea of this; he didn't know how it worked, but was told he didn't need to know. Frank said they had been visiting Earth for years - they liked it as a holiday destination - and that, soon, humans would be travelling to the stars. The aliens would help them with that, when the time came.

Timmy took the crystal and put it in his pocket. Frank said he could walk back out of the building and back up to the surface to enter the passage. When he got back to the surface, he could see the passage and could see the inside of his house. He stepped through the secret tunnel, and with a whoosh, he found himself stood in front of the cupboard under the stairs.

The passage had vanished. It was such a strange experience that Timmy wondered if it had really happened. He put his hand in his pocket. He could feel the crystal. It was real. Timmy went to tell his mum, but when he did, she didn't believe him. She thought he was just making it up and telling a tall tale. Timmy knew it was true, and he knew when the time was right, the passage would open from the crystal and he would meet Frank and the other aliens again.

And when you are ready, you can slowly open your eyes, as *you continue to feel relaxed.*

The Secret Garden

As *you close your eyes*, I'm going to tell you the story about Polly the princess and the secret garden, and with *your eyes closed*, you can listen to me reading this story. While I read this story, you can *begin to feel relaxed*, and as I read, you can *imagine this story* in your mind.

One crisp autumn morning Polly was playing in the garden with her kitten. Suddenly, the kitten ran over to a nearby flowerbed and started digging. Polly wondered what her kitten was doing so she went over to see. She didn't want the kitten digging up the flowerbed; she knew that would make her mum, the queen, angry.

When Polly got over to her kitten, she saw that it was digging up a small metal box. Polly thought this was exciting, so she too started to help dig up the box to see what it was.

Polly's hands - and the kitten's paws - got very dirty as they dug in the ground, but Polly didn't care. She wanted to know what was inside the metal container, so she kept on digging.

Once she had got the box free from the ground, she had to find a way to open it. She always had hair grips in her hair, so she decided to use one of the hair grips to try to pick the lock. Polly carefully slid it into the lock and started to turn it slowly. She held her head close to the lock to try to hear the sound of the lock moving; she also closed her eyes and stuck out her tongue. Somehow, this seemed to help her to concentrate and focus.

The kitten also seemed to become very still and focused on Polly's small fingers carefully holding and jiggling the hair grip in the lock. After a few minutes there was a "pop!" and the lid sprung open.

Inside the metal container was a single rolled-up old sheet of paper. Polly gently removed the paper from the tin, put the tin to one side and started to unroll the paper.

As she unrolled it, she realised it was a map of the palace that she lived in. She recognised the lines showing where the palace was, and circles marking out the big trees in the garden, and lines marking out the paths across the garden. But there was one path on the map she didn't recognise. She had never seen this path in the garden before, and it didn't seem to go anywhere.

Polly tried to work out where the path was. She looked for things she recognised, like trees and paths. She went to the path nearest to the one she couldn't see in the garden.

She looked on the map to see what other landmarks there were that she could use to find the old path. She saw two trees that the path passed between, and another further along that the path used to go alongside.

From this information, she was able to work out where the path was. She started to follow where she thought the path was, not knowing what she would find. To her, it looked like normal garden grass - nothing special.

When she reached where she thought the path ended on the map, she stopped to look around. It looked like the path didn't lead anywhere. She wondered whether that was why someone got rid of the path and planted grass over it. But then she thought, why was the map hidden in a metal box and buried in the garden?

'There has to be something here,' Polly thought to herself. She looked closely at the ground trying to find any clue about what was on this spot.

Polly couldn't find anything, so she sat down on the grass and called over her kitten to play. As she sat down with a thud, she heard a hollow echo beneath her. She pulled up some of the grass to reveal a silver metal lid; as she pulled up more and more, she was able to read the writing on the lid: Secret Garden.

Polly smiled, she had always wanted a secret garden. But then she thought to herself 'underground is a strange place for a secret garden…' She had to lift the lid and find out.

The lid was surprisingly light. She was expecting it to be heavy, or stuck down so that it wouldn't move. Polly lifted the lid and peered inside the tunnel. As soon as it was open, the tunnel lit up. The walls were made of light. Then a small white platform rose up to the top of the tunnel. Polly picked up her kitten and stepped onto the platform.

The platform was like a lift. Once she stood on it, it started to go down, slow and smooth, back into the tunnel. Polly thought she had been in the lift for ages. She felt like it was still moving, but everything around her was white so she wasn't quite sure. Suddenly, the lift appeared above ground again. This confused Polly. She thought she was heading down; how did she end up going up and coming out the top again?

This wasn't the only thing that confused Polly. The garden she had come out of the lift in wasn't her garden. This must be the secret garden. It was definitely a garden she had never seen before. This garden was strange. It was like night-time in this garden. Polly could see stars and colours in the sky. The plants were unusual. They were glowing with different coloured lights; there were purple flowers, pink flowers, red flowers and blue flowers.

Polly could see hummingbirds with shining wings buzzing in and out of the plants, and many glowing insects flying around. Polly thought about how much colour there was, and how beautiful this garden was. It appeared so magical.

As Polly walked around the garden, she noticed that each step she took left a faint pink glowing footprint on the ground. 'This is such a magical place!' Polly thought to herself.

She knew she would have to leave the garden soon. She didn't want her mum to worry about where she was. Polly and her kitten played in the secret garden for a while, before heading back to the lift.

Polly and the kitten stood on the lift, and with a gentle movement, it began to lower down into the bright tunnel. After what seemed like ages, the lift raised her back out into her garden.

She looked around, the sun was shining, birds were singing, and the garden definitely looked like her normal garden. Polly loved that she now had a secret garden she could visit anytime she wanted.

She picked up her kitten, went back into the palace, and after her little adventure, she settled down on the sofa in the main living room, in front of the crackling log fire, and drifted off into a day-dream, looking forward to visiting the secret garden again in the future.

And, when you are ready, you can slowly open your eyes, as *you continue to feel relaxed.*

Saving Prince Charming

As *you close your eyes*, I'm going to tell you the story about Cindy and her unicorn Oracle, and with *your eyes closed*, you can listen to me reading this story. While I read this story, you can *begin to feel relaxed*, and as I read, you can *imagine this story* in your mind.

One day when Cindy was out riding on her unicorn Oracle in a meadow far from the palace she lived in, she heard a noise coming from the woodland running along the edge of the meadow.

"Come on Oracle, let's see what's happening!" Cindy said.

Cindy nudged Oracle gently in the sides with her feet causing Oracle to neigh and start cantering through the meadow towards the woodland.

As they reached the woodland, Oracle slowed down to a trot, before stopping a short distance from the edge of the trees.

"Help, help!" a distressed young male voice called out.

Between the trees, Cindy could see a boy being taken deep into the woods by a dragon. It looked like the prince who lived in a castle a short ride from the meadow. His name was Joe - although Cindy liked to call him Prince Charming, because she liked his floppy blonde hair.

Cindy didn't know what to do. She was just a small girl - she couldn't rescue the prince. Luckily for Cindy, Oracle had the ability to see into both the future and the past. Cindy had an idea.

She turned Oracle around and cantered off to the other side of the meadow where she knew they wouldn't be seen. From here, she told Oracle that she wanted to see into the future. She wanted to see what was going to happen to the prince and where he was being taken.

Cindy placed her hand firmly on Oracle's neck, touching his hair, closed her eyes, and focused. She could feel warmth as a bright white light formed around Oracle and herself. She focused on the warm light passing down through her body, entering her head, down into her shoulders and arms, then into her body, and finally down into her legs and feet.

As the white light passed gently down through her body, Cindy felt more comfortable and relaxed, and she started to count backwards in her mind: from 10, to 9 ... 8 ... 7 ... 6. With each number she said, she felt even more relaxed: 5 ... 4 ... 3 ... 2 ... 1 ... Once she had counted to one, she began to see things in her imagination. She began to see the prince being taken by the dragon deep into the woods to a hidden cave.

There was a waterfall in the cave with a secret opening behind the waterfall. The dragon took the prince into that secret cave and placed him up high on a ledge, from where he was unable to climb down.

Cindy looked further into the future to find out how she could save the prince. She saw a few opportunities where she might be able to sneak in, and get into the secret cave. She could see that the dragon would leave the cave for a while and fly away… This was her chance to help. 'It isn't every day you get to rescue a prince,' she thought to herself.

After Cindy saw what she needed to see, she opened her eyes. She nudged Oracle gently in the sides, and he cantered up into the air on a cloud of light. They rode over the woodland until they were above the cave Cindy had seen in her imagination. She steered Oracle down towards the ground a short distance from the cave, so that she could sneak quietly in and rescue the prince.

Once on the ground, Cindy crept along - keeping low - behind the trees. She knew the dragon wasn't in the cave at the moment, but she was still worried he may return sooner than expected.

Once in the cave, Cindy lit a torch and ran over to the waterfall. To get into the secret cave behind the waterfall Cindy had to climb up the wet and slippery rocks. She clung on as tight as she could and scratched her legs on the rocks as she climbed. It was very hard work, but she managed it.

Once she entered the secret cave she lit another torch; the cave walls sparkled in its dim light. Cindy could see the prince up on the ledge. The prince noticed Cindy and went to call down to her.

"Shh," Cindy said, "I'm here to rescue you."

"But, how? What if the dragon comes back?" the prince replied.

"I know what I'm doing, we need to be quick."

Cindy found a tree trunk. She knew it would reach the prince, but she wasn't strong enough to move it over and up to the ledge. There were some long vines in the cave. Suddenly, Cindy had a plan. She grabbed the vines and threw them up to the prince; he then lowered them down to her, keeping tight hold of one end. When she grabbed the other end, Cindy tied it to the tree trunk.

With all of his strength, the prince pulled the tree trunk across the ground and up to the ledge. Cindy helped too, by pushing as the prince pulled the trunk up. She also helped to keep the tree trunk steady. Eventually, the two of them got the tree trunk in place. The prince climbed down, and thanked Cindy. He asked her how they were going to escape.

Cindy and the prince could hear the dragon returning to the cave - its wings were noisy as they flapped, and it landed with an earth-rumbling thud. Cindy and the prince made it out of the secret cave and hid behind a rock in the main cave. It was pitch black. Cindy and the prince couldn't see anything, but they could hear the dragon's breathing.

The dragon was walking towards the back of the cave to the waterfall. Cindy worried how the dragon was going to react when it realised the prince was gone. The beast effortlessly jumped up into the secret cave and let out a deafening roar. Fire erupted from inside the secret cave bursting through the waterfall.

Cindy and the prince held their breath. Her heart was beating so hard that she worried the dragon would be able to hear it and discover where they were hidden. She closed her eyes, held on to the prince, and focused on breathing slowly and deeply for a minute or two to help her *relax and focus*.

'Breathe in ... and breathe out ... that's it ... breathe in ... and breathe out ...' Cindy told herself.

After a few minutes, they could hear the dragon walk past them and leave the cave. It seemed to think that Cindy and the prince had already escaped, and it was looking for them. After the dragon left the cave, Cindy and the prince very quietly and carefully followed. It felt good to see sunlight and breathe in fresh air.

Outside the cave, Cindy called to Oracle who appeared out of the trees. She told the prince to get onto Oracle; they had to get the prince back to his castle and let the king and queen know their son was safe. Cindy thought to herself that they would be surprised to see him saved by a small girl.

Cindy gently squeezed Oracle with her feet, causing him to leap up into the sky on a rainbow and gallop off towards the castle.

At the castle, the king and queen were so happy to see their son. As they entered, the queen wrapped him up in her arms so tight that the prince thought his eyes might pop out of his head. The king was also pleased to see his son. He wanted to send his finest knights out to fight the dragon. Cindy explained that the dragon was just doing what dragons do, but that the important thing was that the prince was safe - they had their son back.

Cindy didn't believe animals or people should be harmed, even the dragon. She told the king that there was only one dragon in the land, so it should be looked after. The king agreed. He put in place a plan to look after the dragon that would stop it from harming anyone again.

The prince thanked Cindy for saving him. He hoped he would see her again in the future. Cindy was sure they would see each other. She called Oracle over, climbed onto his back, gave him a nudge in his sides, and they rode off into the sky on a bright and colourful sparkling rainbow, looking forward to their next adventure.

And when you are ready, you can slowly open your eyes, as *you continue to feel relaxed.*

Jonny's Rotten Apple

As *you close your eyes*, I'm going to tell you the story about Jonny's rotten apple, and with *your eyes closed*, you can listen to me reading this story. While I read this story, you can *begin to feel relaxed*, and as I read, you can *imagine this story* in your mind.

One birthday, Jonny's favourite uncle gave him an apple. "This is a special apple, Jonny. Whatever you do, don't take a bite out of it; this apple is going to bring you good luck," he said.

Jonny liked eating apples, so he didn't know how he was going to manage to not eat this apple. It was a beautiful green apple. Just thinking about biting into the apple had Jonny's mouth watering. He could imagine what it would feel like to bite into that apple, what it would sounds like as his teeth crunched through the green skin and into the juicy sweet goodness inside.

"Thank you, uncle Dave," Jonny replied, "I will try not to eat the apple."

"Remember Jonny, don't eat it. It is going to bring you good luck."

Jonny was confused by his uncle Dave's insistence about the apple. 'Is it really that important that I don't eat the apple?' Jonny thought to himself. 'Couldn't I just go and get another apple if I eat this one? Can one apple really bring good luck?'

Jonny didn't know what to do with the apple. He thought to himself, if the apple was supposed to bring good luck, perhaps he should keep the apple on him all the time. He didn't know how it was supposed to bring him good luck - whether it was going to bring him one bit of good luck or lots of good luck.

Jonny asked his mum for a plastic box to put the apple in so that he could keep it in his school bag. She gave him a square white milk-coloured box, with a blue lid which clipped down around the outside to hold it in place. Jonny put the apple into the box, and put the box in his bag.

Every day, before Jonny went to school, he checked that the box was still in his bag. After a couple of weeks, Jonny was so used to having the box in his bag that he often forgot it was even in there. He hadn't noticed it bring him good luck yet, but he didn't think his uncle Dave would be wrong.

After a couple of weeks, Jonny had forgotten about the box. It had sunk to the bottom of his school bag, and every day, he stuffed everything into his bag on top of the box, without paying any attention to it - or to the apple.

One day on the way into school, some bullies were calling Jonny horrible names. He tried to ignore them and kept walking, but he was getting upset by what they were saying. The bullies started calling Jonny names every day as he walked to school, and he kept ignoring them. It didn't seem to make them stop. Jonny wondered whether he should tell his parents, or a teacher… He didn't know what they would be able to do, or whether they would even make it worse by talking with the bullies.

After a couple of weeks of being called names by the bullies and not reacting to what they were saying, they began to push Jonny around. Jonny continued to try to ignore them but he was both scared and angry at the same time.

After school one day he told his mum about the bullies. His mum comforted him and asked if he would like her to do anything to help. Jonny told his mum that he felt better because he had spoken to her, and that he would continue to try to ignore them. Hopefully, he thought, they would get bored and then leave him alone.

His mum felt this was a good idea. She knew that if she got involved at this stage it could make things worse for Jonny, but it was important that he spoke to her; then, if the situation got worse or continued much longer, she could get involved.

After a few more days of the bullies picking on Jonny and pushing him around, they demanded his packed lunch. "I've eaten it," Jonny replied honestly.

The bullies took Jonny's bag, unzipped it and emptied everything on the ground.

"No you haven't, you liar!" one of the bullies said as they saw the plastic tub fall to the ground in a way that made it obvious there was something inside.

"That's mine, it's not my lunch!" Jonny said.

The bullies didn't believe him. They started passing the tub between themselves. Jonny tried to grab the tub, but the bullies were too big. "Give that back, it's mine!" he shouted.

The bullies laughed, they didn't want to give it back. They had spent weeks trying to find a way of getting a reaction from Jonny, and now, they wanted to make the most of it. Jonny was annoyed with them; he wasn't scared, or angry - just annoyed that they had taken something that didn't belong to them.

This wasn't the reaction the bullies wanted, but it was better than no reaction at all. Jonny knew that most bullies needed a reaction to keep them interested in bullying someone. They normally want the person they are bullying to be scared of them, or to get angry and try to fight them, but to be too small or weak to be any real threat to them.

Jonny wasn't going to try to fight them, and he wasn't going to be scared of them, but he was getting annoyed with them. He focused on breathing calmly and not reacting to the bullies. He wanted his tub back but he wasn't going to let the bullies win by getting emotional in front of them.

"Pass it here," the leader of the bullies said, "I'm going to have your lunch."

The bully took the tub from one of his friends and grabbed the fold-down clips around the side of the tub. As he popped them open, the lid exploded off of the tub and rotten apple squirted in his face.

The bully spat the apple out as he threw the tub on the ground. The other bullies and children gathered around all started to laugh. The bully ran off, embarrassed.

Jonny had forgotten about the apple over the last few weeks, he didn't realise how rotten it would have gotten in the tub; as it got more rotten, it gave off more gas which increased inside the tub but had nowhere to go. The pressure built up and exploded out when it was finally opened. Jonny was glad he didn't open the tub.

The next day, the bullies avoided Jonny, they didn't even look at him. Jonny thought to himself: 'That apple really did bring me good luck.' He didn't know how his uncle Dave knew it was going to bring him good luck, but he was very happy that he was given that lucky apple.

And when you are ready, you can slowly open your eyes, as *you continue to feel relaxed.*

The Curious Discovery

As *you close your eyes*, I'm going to tell you the story about Taylor the swift and Lucy the swallow's curious discovery, and with *your eyes closed*, you can listen to me reading this story. While I read this story, you can *begin to feel relaxed*. And as I read, you can *imagine this story* in your mind.

Every evening, just as the sun sets, Taylor the swift darts around high up in the sky, grabbing a bite to eat. As she does this, she is in a great position to see what else is going on in the evening.

One day, while Taylor was flying high above the village, she noticed something unusual. She saw a funny shape in the sky, followed by flashes of light. Then, she saw something falling out of the sky off in the distance, landing somewhere behind the faraway trees. Taylor was intrigued by this, so she flew to her friend Lucy the swallow.

"Did you see something in the sky which was bright and odd-looking? It flashed and dropped out of the sky landing somewhere off in the distance…" Taylor asked Lucy

"No, what did it look like?"

"I don't know, it was bright and flashing, and it looked big, but seemed to be different shapes," Taylor tried to recall what it looked like as she described it, "We should go and investigate, and try to find it."

Lucy agreed. It sounded like fun trying to find whatever had landed.

As they started their journey towards whatever had fallen, they wondered how far they would have to travel. All they knew was that it had landed somewhere the other side of the woodland. It was going to be a long journey.

"What do you think it was?" Lucy asked.

"I don't know... Maybe it was a spaceship landing. It was travelling down to land very fast."

"Or maybe it was a new fast human plane landing?" replied Lucy.

They were both curious, and neither one knew what it could be. They had heard humans talking about spaceships before, and how they had seen spaceships in the sky, but Taylor and Lucy didn't believe this. 'But if it wasn't a spaceship, what could it be?' they wondered...

By the time they reached the woodland, the sun had set and the moon and stars had begun to rise. The air seemed to change - it felt calm and cool. As darkness set in, everything also seemed much quieter. Lucy and Taylor were normally tucked up warm at home at this time of day. They noticed how calm, peaceful and relaxing it was to be flying on a summer's evening after the sun had set.

Eventually, Taylor and Lucy had flown beyond the woodland. They didn't know what they were looking for. Lucy suggested they fly up higher to get a better view of the area and to try to spot the object.

From up high, everything looked so small. They could see the moonlight sparkling and twinkling on the water of a lake, giving everything a comforting glow. Taylor thought about how everything during the day can be so full of colour, whereas at night it is all different shades of blue.

After flying for what seemed like ages, Taylor spotted something on the ground in a field. "Look! Over there! There is something white in that field."

Lucy and Taylor flew closer for a look. Taylor couldn't land on the ground because, as a swift, she only had short legs, so Lucy flew down to investigate.

She peeked at the white object. It appeared to be made of lightweight white metal poles, some of which seemed to have been damaged in the landing. There was also a box with odd looking symbols printed on it, and inside the box were unusual-looking tubes, and electronics. Attached to what Lucy thought must be the top of the object were thin white strings, leading to what looked like a giant burst balloon.

"What do you think it is?" Lucy asked Taylor.

"I don't know… It looks like a balloon which was carrying something."

Lucy knew someone who would know what the object was. He seemed to know everything. He had been around for a very long time. He was much older than Lucy or Taylor, or anyone else they knew - he was Harry the parrot. Harry had been living with humans in their houses for so long; he would know what it must be.

Lucy and Taylor flew back to the village to find Harry. They found his house and tapped on the window. All the lights were off now, as it was late and all of the humans had gone to bed. Suddenly, Harry appeared at the window.

He didn't often have visitors, so he was excited to see Lucy and Taylor.

"Harry, we need your help! Something has fallen out of the sky. It is a curious object, and we don't know what it is, or what it was for," Lucy said

In an aged, deep and slow voice, Harry replied: "I'll be right there."

Harry had lived in the house for a long time and knew how to get out. Within what seemed like seconds, he was perched beside Lucy on the windowsill. She didn't know how he got there so quickly - she didn't ask. All three of the birds flew off back to the object.

Harry took a look at the object making 'umming' and 'ahhing' sounds. He was obviously thinking hard about what the object might be and what it was for, and why it had fallen from the sky.

"It's easy, this object is a weather balloon," Harry said.

"What's a weather balloon?" asked Taylor.

"A weather balloon is something humans use to find out information about the weather."

"Can't they look at the sky, like we do?" Lucy replied.

"Humans like to understand the weather, now and in the past, to try to work out what it will be like in the future too. They add gas lighter than air to a balloon until it starts to rise on its own, then they let it go. It goes all the way up, nearly to space, but as it goes up higher and higher the balloon gets bigger and bigger, until it is so big it pops and everything falls back to the ground. The box has instruments in for measuring the weather at different heights in the sky so that the humans can work out what the weather is like. From that, they can see how the weather will be in the future."

Taylor and Lucy were intrigued by this. They thought it was fascinating that this balloon had nearly been to space and now they could touch it.

It was getting late, so Taylor, Lucy and Harry flew back to the village, went back to their homes, and that night, they all went to sleep dreaming about what it must be like to fly almost all the way up to space.

And when you are ready, you can slowly open your eyes, as *you continue to feel relaxed.*

The Butterfly and the Bee

As *you close your eyes*, I'm going to tell you the story about Robin the butterfly and his friend Henry the bee, and with *your eyes closed*, you can listen to me reading this story. While I read this story, you can *begin to feel relaxed*. And as I read, you can *imagine this story* in your mind.

Robin hadn't been a butterfly long when he was drinking some nectar from a plant one day, and a bee came buzzing along to the same flower. While Robin drank, he looked over at the bee. The bee looked very busy, it was flying in and out of all the flowers. Robin noticed that the bee was getting all dirty - every time he flew into a flower he came out with more sticky yellow bits all over his legs and back.

"Excuse me," Robin began, "excuse me!" The bee was so busy it didn't seem to notice Robin calling. "Hello, Mr Bee!" Robin shouted.

The bee landed next to Robin. "Can I help you?" the bee asked.

"What are you doing? It looks like very dirty work; you are getting yellow dirt all over you."

"I'm gathering pollen and nectar."

"What is all the yellow dirt you are getting all over your legs and back?" Robin asked curiously.

"That is pollen. It helps the plants survive, and helps feed my family."

Robin didn't understand. he wanted to know how it helped the plants survive. The bee explained that the pollen rubbed off on him as he entered the plants, he carried it to the next plant, where he would crawl in, and the pollen would rub off. He said it helped plants have children. The bee saw this as something he did as payment for being allowed the nectar - the plants also allowed him to take away some of the pollen as well.

"I'm Robin, by the way."

"I'm Henry," replied the bee.

"I used to be a caterpillar, now I'm a butterfly. I've not been a butterfly for long, so I'm learning lots of new things. What do you do with the pollen and nectar?" Robin asked.

"Come back to my home with me and I will show you."

Robin went with Henry back to Henry's home. As they approached, Robin could see how busy and chaotic it looked with hundreds of bees buzzing around flying in and out of a hole in a tree. The closer they got, the noisier it got.

"Here we are!" Henry said, "This is home."

Robin was curious. He landed as close as he could to the entrance and tried to peer in. It was very dark inside the hole. Henry went over to one of the bees and passed it some nectar. The bee ate some of it before passing it on to another bee, and that bee passed it on to another, and so on. Robin was curious about this. He could see that each bee was eating some of the pollen and nectar before sharing it with others. Robin noticed that the nectar food started out watery, but became less watery as each bee had some to eat. After the last bee had eaten some, and the food was getting dry, the bee placed it in a hole, and sealed the hole with some wax.

"What was that the last bee placed in the hole?"

"That was honey," Henry replied. "Once the liquid starts to get thick we store it as sweet, healthy food for the future."

Robin had never seen where bees lived before, and had never heard of honey. He wanted to know what the honey tasted like.

It was dark in the bees' home. Henry told Robin that there was a place where he would be able to see into a bees' home. He told Robin the home is called a hive. Henry and Robin flew to a nearby field where a man in a funny white suit covering his whole body and face was spraying smoke into some white boxes.

Henry and Robin flew close to one of the boxes, keeping just out of the smoke. "Look, Robin!" Henry said as the man in the white suit lifted the lid from one of the boxes and raised something covered in bees up out of the box.

Robin looked as the man sprayed smoke on the bees. This made some fly away, and others seemed to *become really relaxed*. He saw golden-coloured hexagons all with wax lids. The man in the funny white suit had a device which pushed the honey out of the hexagons. As honey poured out of the machine it glistened and sparkled in the sunlight.

Henry suggested that Robin went and had a taste of the honey. So he did. He flew over to the large pot of gloopy honey and had a drink. He thought to himself how tasty the honey was. He didn't have any way of making this. He thought to himself how magical bees were, being able to work together to make something so tasty.

Henry flew over with a container of honey, "Here, I've got you some honey to take home with you."

Robin felt so lucky. He had only just met Henry and he was already being so kind. As the sun set over the meadow, Henry and Robin said goodbye to each other. Henry went back to his hive, and Robin went home with his pot of honey and a feeling that this had been a good day.

And, in your own time, you can slowly open your eyes, as *you continue to feel relaxed.*

The Clown Who Never Grew Up

As *you close your eyes*, I'm going to tell you the story about James and his first circus adventure, and with *your eyes closed*, you can listen to me reading this story. While I read this story, you can *begin to feel relaxed*. And as I read, you can *imagine this story* in your mind.

Every circus contains strange tales of wonder and intrigue, and the circus James joined was no different. On James' first day in the circus, he saw a young-looking clown. But he had been told that he was the youngest person in the circus, so he was curious as to who this clown was. The clown never took off his make-up, and he never spoke to other circus staff.

James followed the clown around and tried to keep an eye on him. He had tried to talk to the clown, but the clown ignored him and just carried on walking around. James hadn't seen the clown doing any work, all he seemed to do was walk around the circus *slowly and calmly*.

Although this person was dressed as a clown, he didn't seem very funny; he didn't really act like a clown. James decided to talk with some of the circus staff about the clown. He asked one of the jugglers, but the juggler said he didn't know the clown - he had never seen him.

James went and asked some of the acrobats, and they too said they had never seen or met this clown. He thought perhaps he should ask the other clowns - he thought they would know who this clown was. But they didn't. They all said they didn't know who the clown was, and they had never met him at all.

This was getting confusing for James. 'How can no-one know this clown?' he thought to himself. He knew he wasn't imagining the clown... He had followed him around all day.

James went to the owner. He thought, 'If anyone is going to know who works on the circus, he will know, because he would have been the person who hired them.' When James spoke to the owner, the owner's face went white.

"We don't have any young clowns here. What does the clown look like?" the owner said, sounding slightly nervous.

James described what the clown looked like, described how he looked like a child in a homemade clown outfit. He had a white face, and round red foam nose, and green curly hair with a red and yellow hat, and big red shoes.

The owner started to sweat as he walked to a filing cabinet. He opened the cabinet, rummaged around for a few moments before pulling out an old faded newspaper cutting.

"Is that what the boy looked like?" the owner asked as he showed James the newspaper.

On the newspaper was a story about a boy who visited the circus about fifty years ago. There was a photograph of the boy in his clown outfit which his mum had made him. She had taken the photograph of her son just before they left for the circus. The article spoke about the boy going missing at the circus, and he had never been seen since.

The owner told James that the boy had never been found but children who'd visited the circus over the years had spoken about seeing a boy walking around the circus - yet no adults seemed able to see him.

James wondered what had happened to the boy. He wanted to find out, but the only way to find out was to find the boy and make contact with him.

It didn't take long for James to spot the boy walking around the outside of the main circus tent. James approached him. "Are you the boy who went missing 50 years ago?" James asked.

The boy turned to face James, and nodded his head slowly with a sad look on his face.

"Can you talk to me?" James asked.

The boy shook his head slowly from side to side.

"Can you let me know what happened to you?"

The boy nodded slowly, before turning and walking away. James followed.

The boy walked slowly around the outside of the main circus tent, past a ring toss stand, and a hook-a-duck game too. No-one else noticed the boy James was following. He continued following the boy around a corner, leading James to a fortune telling machine.

The boy stopped at the machine, staring into the eyes of the fortune teller in the machine. James stood next to the boy. "I don't understand…" James said.

He didn't understand why the boy had just stopped and stared at the fortune teller in the machine. It wasn't a real person. The fortune teller was made of wood. It was an inanimate object. After a few minutes of staring with the boy, James turned to him once again. "I don't understand…"

The boy turned his head to look at James before pulling out a small piece of paper, unfolding it and showing it to him.

'Your wish is granted' was written on the paper.

"Did you make a wish?"

The boy nodded.

James wondered what wish the boy had made. He wondered how he could find out. He couldn't see how making a wish could be linked with the boy now being a ghost.

"Is your disappearance linked to the wish you made?" James asked.

The boy nodded again.

James decided that he needed to find out more about the fortune telling machine. It worked by putting a coin in the slot, making a wish, then pressing a red button on the front of the machine. Once that button was pressed, the wooden fortune teller moved his arm and head, as something was written on a note. A few moments later, the note dropped into a slot at the bottom of the machine for the customer to have.

James hadn't been around the circus for long, but he had been there long enough to know that the fortune telling machine didn't really grant wishes or tell people their fortune. He had seen the circus staff put the notes into the machine every day; there was nothing special about them.

James went back to the circus offices. He wanted to find out more about this machine. He wanted to know where it came from and how long it had been around.

James found the documents about the machine. He read that the machine was made in 1745 by a clock maker called Johann Rasputin. He made the clockwork fortune teller because he wanted to find out what life he was going to have in the future. He believed that he could make a fortune teller, use a magic ritual, and the fortune teller would become real.

This was the kind of common belief that many people held back in the 1700s, so James didn't think anything of this, but he wanted to know what happened next. How did the fortune teller end up in the circus?

James searched on the internet to see if there was any information about Johann Rasputin and his clockwork fortune teller. He found details showing that, in 1829, the fortune teller was in an auction and the circus founder purchased it for this new circus he was starting.

He found records showing that there had been other news stories about this fortune teller before - about strange events, people claiming they made wishes which had been granted. James noticed that everyone who seemed to have had their wishes granted believed 100% that the fortune teller was genuinely able to grant their wishes.

He found a news article about the disappearance of the boy he had been following. In the article, his mother described their day up to her son's disappearance. She described how she had just taken him to see the circus animals, and then they went to the fortune teller machine where he wished that he could stay in the circus forever. After a few minutes of the fortune teller moving its head and arm, out popped the piece of paper: 'Your wish is granted'.

She looked at this with her son, he put the paper in his pocket, held her hand, and they walked towards the circus tent to go and watch the next show which was due to start shortly. It was very busy in the queue to get into the circus tent. She'd let go of her son's hand for a moment so that she could show the tickets to the staff at the entrance to the tent. When she reached back down to take hold of her son's hand, he was no longer there.

She thought he had got lost in the crowds, and since that day, she had never known what had happened to him. James thought he now knew what had happened. Until now he had never believed that the fortune teller was real.

James thought that the boy's wish really had been granted - that when his mother let go of his hand, his wish had come true. He had vanished and became a ghost, destined to roam around the circus forever, never growing up, and never being able to leave.

James had an idea about how he may be able to help, too. The boy looked so sad; he didn't like the idea of this boy having to be alone like this forever.

James went back to the fortune teller machine, the boy still stood next to it. James put a coin into the machine.

"I wish the boy's wish was never granted" he wished. He then pushed the red button.

The fortune teller started to whir and move its head and arm. After a few moments, a slip of paper dropped out of the machine. James picked it up. 'Your wish is granted.'

James turned to the boy, the boy was looking back at James, then gradually he began to fade away. As he faded away, James noticed the boy was starting to smile.

Just as the boy disappeared, James jumped as he felt a hand on his shoulder. It was an adult man's hand. He turned around, startled.

"You've just seen a young boy dressed as a clown disappear, haven't you?" the man asked.

"Yes?" James said wondering how this man knew.

"That boy was me. Fifty years ago, I made a wish and it came true. I remember everything. I remember being trapped in this circus for fifty years. When you made your wish for me, I disappeared and reappeared back in my body fifty years ago as if my wish hadn't been granted, but I had all the memories of the fifty years I was trapped here. Nothing changed for anyone else. I made sure to remember that, in fifty years' time, I needed to come to this circus at this very moment, to find you and thank you for your help."

The man thanked James and told him that he knew how to stop the fortune teller granting wishes for real in the future. James and the man made the changes to the fortune teller, so that no one else would have such a bad experience again.

When James tried telling people his story, no-one believed him. All the records about the boy disappearing had vanished. James was glad he had got his job at the circus. More importantly, though, he was glad he had not found the machine and made the same wish himself.

And when you are ready, you can slowly open your eyes, as *you continue to feel relaxed.*

The Early Worm Catches the Bird

As *you close your eyes*, I'm going to tell you the story about Sid the time-travelling worm, and with *your eyes closed*, you can listen to me reading this story. While I read this story, you can *begin to feel relaxed*. And as I read, you can *imagine this story* in your mind.

Sid was an unusual worm. When he made wormholes, they led to different times and places. Other worms would tunnel from one part of a garden to another, but Sid would tunnel from one time to another. He didn't have control over where his wormholes would lead, so he had to keep track of each hole he dug so that he could find his way around - not just in space, but in time, too.

One day, Sid dug a tunnel from his garden. Halfway through his tunnel, the ground started to shake. Sid didn't know what was happening. Was this an earthquake, or something else? As Sid poked his head out of the tunnel, he noticed a shadow moving towards him. He looked up and saw a giant grey foot about to come down on his head.

Sid quickly slid back into his wormhole as the giant foot crashed down, sending a shockwave through the ground. After the shaking calmed down, Sid burrowed back to the wormhole exit. He looked back to see what the animal was with big feet, and he saw a diplodocus walking away from him. Sid realised that he had travelled back in time to the time of the dinosaurs.

Sid slithered out of his wormhole to go and explore this time. He had to make sure he could keep track of his wormhole; if he lost the wormhole he would have to burrow again, and each time he burrowed, he could come out at any time and place, so getting home would be unlikely. He was confident he could find his wormhole this time, though, because it was in the middle of a giant footprint.

There is a rule in time travel, that you should never interfere with the time you are in, because even the smallest interference can have a huge impact in the future. Sid always tried not to interfere with the past, but he found this difficult. Because his life was spent time-travelling, he couldn't remember exactly what time period he initially lived in - and there were many different time periods he liked. So, because he had lived in the present and the future, he was aware that everything he did in the present could impact on the future he liked, and his awareness of the future could make him make different decisions in the present, which would then change the future. It was very complicated - so complicated, in fact, that Sid decided to *forget all about it and relax*. He just tried to lead his life not interfering with time. So far, everything seemed to be going okay.

The diplodocus had left a trail of destruction where it had been. There were trees uprooted and broken in half, and footprints like craters covered the ground. Sid saw what looked like a bird's nest in a tree. It was obviously a nest of a small bird-like dinosaur rather than an actual bird, but it was probably a distant relative of future birds. The nest had been damaged by the dinosaur as it walked past, with one of the eggs falling out and breaking on the ground.

Sid thought about how sad this was, but there was nothing he could have done. The mother dino-bird was sat on her nest, trying to keep what was left of her eggs safe. She looked a bit like a dinosaur but had fine, soft, fluffy feathers all over her body, with what looked like scales, like on chicken's feet, over her body just under the soft layer of feathers. On her arms, too, were larger, colourful feathers, looking almost like they had just been stuck on.

Sid was intrigued by this dino-bird, and so he watched it for a while. It didn't seem to be able to fly as such, but it could climb trees with its claws, and it could jump out of trees and glide by stretching out its wings. Sid thought about how there was still some way to go before this dinobird was likely to become a bird.

After enjoying some time watching and learning about dinosaurs and about this dino-bird, Sid decided to continue his exploring. He went back to his wormhole, and started to burrow a hole right next to his first hole. He always burrowed new holes next to his old holes, so that he could easily find his way back from hole to hole.

When Sid exited his wormhole this time, to his surprise, he didn't seem to have travelled in time. Everything outside of the hole looked the same. As he looked closer, he noticed he was wrong. Everything looked roughly the same, but everything wasn't exactly the same. It looked like he had come out in almost the same location, everything was familiar, but the damage done by the diplodocus hadn't happened. His previous wormhole hadn't appeared yet - the nest in the tree was still in the tree, intact.

Sid could feel the ground rumbling with each step of the diplodocus, and could see its grey figure in the distance coming towards him. He had never been in this position before, one where he knew the immediate outcome of what was going to happen, and he knew he had a choice he could make which would have a direct impact on the future. He didn't spend his time overthinking it, but he had always tried not to do anything which could obviously change the future. This time, though, he knew if he did nothing but watch, then one of the eggs from the nest would get destroyed. Maybe, somehow, he would be able to save the egg.

Sid had to make a quick decision: whether to save the egg or not. If he was going to save the egg, he had to decide how. Sid decided that he couldn't knowingly let the egg get destroyed. He had to find a way of trying to save it. He didn't have long. The dinosaur was getting closer and closer.

Sid knew exactly where the egg was going to fall. It didn't look like the egg was stood on - the tree was damaged and the egg just fell onto the solid ground, cracking open on impact. Sid had a plan, but he had to work fast. He slithered over to where the egg was going to fall, and instead of digging a wormhole like he normally would, he churned up the top soil in a circle the size of a dinner plate. He did this a few centimetres deep so that that bit of mud would be softer to land on. He could hear the dinosaur's footsteps getting louder as it got closer.

Next, Sid started grabbing leaves and dragging them over to his churned-up mud. He piled the leaves up on top of each other to create a crashmat for the egg to fall on to. Once he had finished creating the leafy crashmat, he wrote next to it: 'From you, to you – you built this leafy crashmat here. When you go through your next wormhole make sure you build this.'

The diplodocus was very close now. Sid quickly moved himself out of the way. When the dinosaur was just a couple of steps away, he saw himself popping up out of his first wormhole, then suddenly seeing the dinosaur foot, and so ducking back into the wormhole. The foot came down with a thud, the ground shook, the dinosaur gave a couple more ground-shaking steps as it passed by, hitting the nest with its swinging tail and knocking the egg from its perch.

The egg fell to the ground, landing safely on Sid's leafy crashmat. The dinosaur continued walking into the distance. Sid popped back down his wormhole, pleased with himself. He was aware that when he popped up from his first wormhole, he would now see the egg on the bed of leaves, and so wouldn't think about having to build that leafy crashmat. The message he left himself would solve the time-travelling paradox he otherwise would have created, where he would have gone back into the past, built the leafy crashmat, saved the egg, then appeared again. He would have seen the egg was on a leafy crashmat, gone back into the past, not thought to build the crashmat (because the egg was fine) so the egg would not land on a crashmat. So, when he appeared, he would see the smashed egg, and build the crashmat.

Sid thought to himself that this was too much to get his head around, even as a skilled time-travelling worm. So, by writing a message to himself, he would then ensure he built the crashmat, and would know he was the one responsible for the crashmat he could see.

Sid wondered whether anything else had changed. When he got back to the present, he was pleased to see that the only thing which seemed to have changed was a new, colourful species of bird which hadn't existed before.

He decided that it had been such a long day, with trying to work out time-travelling paradoxes, that he settled down in his garden, closed his eyes, and took a long nap.

And when you are ready, you can slowly open your eyes, as *you continue to feel relaxed.*

Patches in the Dog House

As *you close your eyes*, I'm going to tell you the story about Patches the puppy, and with *your eyes closed*, you can listen to me reading this story. While I read this story, you can *begin to feel relaxed*. And as I read, you can *imagine this story* in your mind.

One day, Patches was playing inside the house. He was trying to see how fast he could jump from each item of furniture. He had a route he was trying to follow to do laps around the living room. Patches jumped from one arm of the sofa to the other arm, then over onto the armchair, then from the armchair to the foot stool, then over to the bean bag, then up onto a dining room chair, then onto another, and another, then up onto the dining room table.

This was as far as Patches could easily get. Up to this point, he could jump very fast from one place to another. But he had to *now slow down*, as he thought about how he was going to complete his course. He had to jump from the dining room table up onto the bookcase, then carefully make his way along the bookcase without knocking anything off, before jumping over to the fireplace. The fireplace was even more difficult to walk along. There were framed photographs of the family, a clock, some artificial candles, and a bunch of flowers in a vase which he was going to have to navigate. The fireplace shelf was also very narrow.

Patches carefully leapt over onto the shelf. There was barely enough room for his tiny paws to fit. He nearly slipped and fell. Patches held his breath for a moment to try to *be as still as possible*. Once he had got his balance, he *gently let that breath out, and relaxed*.

"Patches, what are you doing in there?" a voice shouted from the kitchen. Clearly, the mother of the family which owned Patches had heard all of the noise he was making as he jumped around the living room.

Patches *stayed still and relaxed*. He thought to himself that if he *stayed still and quiet,* the mother would stop paying attention to him, and would get on with whatever she was doing in the kitchen.

This seemed to work. A minute or two passed, which to Patches felt like an hour, and the mother hadn't come through to the living room - or even shouted again. Patches took this as a sign that he could continue to play his game.

To jump from the shelf above the fireplace to the top of the television, Patches first had to carefully make his way along the shelf. This wasn't easy. He had to stretch and bend his body around the pictures, the candles, the clock and the vase of flowers.

This was his second lap around the room, so he knew he could do it, but he had to focus and concentrate. He carefully arched his body around the first picture, inadvertently dusting the picture with his fur as he brushed past. He managed to get past the first candle easily, just as he had done before; passing the clock was fine too, as he was able to step over this. The next candle was trickier, but Patches was proud of himself for managing to pass that, and he passed the second picture fine. The most challenging part of walking along the shelf was passing the flowers in the vase.

Patches had passed the flowers before on his first lap, but nearly knocked them down as he passed. The vase was quite wide and the flowers caught on his fur. He tried to slide past again; as he did he could feel the flowers tickling his back. They made his tail flick up just as he was jumping off the shelf.

Smash.

The vase hit the floor, shattering and leaving a puddle of water, broken glass, and flowers.

"PATCHES!!!" the mother shouted from the kitchen.

Patches could hear the mother stomping towards the living room. As she entered, he looked up at her with his tail between his legs, and his eyes wide and apologetic.

"Go to your dog house," the mother said, firmly. She pointed out through the kitchen towards the back garden, signalling for Patches to leave the house. Patches walked slowly through the house keeping his tail between his legs. The mother opened the back door for him and pointed to his dog house. He walked across the garden and into his dog house, turned around a few times and sat down resting his head on his front paws.

Patches didn't like being told off. He knew he had broken something and so there should be consequences, but that didn't make it feel any better.

While he sat silently in his dog house, he listened to the sounds in the garden, sounds of birds singing, squirrels scampering, and trees rustling. As he listened to all the different sounds, his mind started to wander. He started to think about how he could play his game without getting told off. He enjoyed running around and having fun, he thought to himself whether he could set the game up in the garden.

Being in his dog house gave Patches a chance to think about his behaviour and what he could do differently next time. When the mother returned, and told him he could now leave the dog house, he decided to set up a course around the garden like the one in the living room, but hopefully without getting into trouble.

Patches looked at the mother with a big grin, sticking his bottom in the air and wagging his tail.

"Would you like me to help you to make a course outside?" the mother asked.

Patches barked and turned around.

The mother and Patches created a course outside using some cushions to jump onto like islands, and broomsticks to make narrow paths to carefully follow.

Patches enjoyed his new course, and knew he wouldn't get told off or break anything as he ran around it. He played in his new course all afternoon until he was tired out. Once he was tired and felt he had had enough, he went back inside and settled down in his comfy dog basket, and had a nap.

And when you are ready, you can slowly open your eyes, as *you continue to feel relaxed.*

Milton's Magical Mystery Tour

As *you close your eyes*, I'm going to tell you the story of Milton and his magical mystery tour, and with *your eyes closed*, you can listen to me reading this story. While I read this story, you can *begin to feel relaxed*. And as I read, you can *imagine this story* in your mind.

Milton loved to sleep. He loved to sleep, because he loved to dream. Dreams were his chance to experience strange and interesting worlds. Milton didn't just dream at night, though; he often found himself *drifting off into a dream* during the day. He loved to day-dream.

One day when Milton was in a history class in school, learning about ancient Egypt and how the pyramids were built, he found himself gazing out of the window into the school playground. As he watched the roundabout slowly turning in the wind, and dry autumn leaves blowing past the window, his *mind began to wander*. He started to *imagine* that the autumn leaves were like the dry sand blowing across a barren desert, and the roundabout was a wheel, with rope being wound and unwound by builders, rotating it to drag huge stones into position to be worked on and shaped.

As Milton allowed himself to *become absorbed deeper* in his day-dream, he could hear the sounds of the people speaking, and the clatter of hammers and chisels against the stone blocks. He could see the school playground disappearing as a new reality started to appear outside, one of ancient Egypt. The last thing to disappear was the window he was looking out of, and the school building, and then the teacher's voice, which gradually faded away into the background.

Milton was now *fully absorbed* in his day-dream. Even though his body was going to stay exactly where it was in reality, in the classroom, in his dream he could get up and move around, and to Milton everything felt totally real.

In his day-dreams, just like in his night-time dreams, time was different. Hours or days could pass in his dream world, but he could find that only minutes had passed in the real world. Sometimes it was just seconds.

Milton had drifted into a day-dream in class many times in the past, and sometimes he had found that only a couple of seconds of real-world time had passed, but to him, he had just been off on an adventure for days in a dream-world.

Within his dream-world, Milton stood up and started to walk towards the men who were turning the large heavy-looking wheel where the roundabout once was. As he walked towards the wheel, he could feel the warmth of the sun on his skin. The sun seemed to be getting warmer with each step that he took. Every moment took Milton *deeper* into his experience.

He had often wondered why he seemed to day-dream so much in school lessons, and he decided it was because it helped him to learn better. When he lived what he was being taught, he found it easier to remember than just hearing a teacher talking about something.

Milton walked among the Egyptians, looking at what they were all doing. There were people dragging giant stones into an area, ready to be shaped; others were shaping the stones to different shapes and sizes depending on where they were going to be used; others were dragging the stones to where the pyramid was being built.

"Young lad!" a man called out. "Excuse me, young lad!"

Milton looked around to see who was calling. There was a friendly-looking man wearing white clothes that looked like they kept him very cool. He had a big, kind smile and was looking straight at Milton. Milton guessed he must want to talk to him.

"Yes?" Milton replied curiously.

"I'm the caretaker here, would you like me to show you around?"

Milton thought that would be great. If he got shown around, maybe he could learn what everyone was doing. The caretaker started by describing what Milton already knew. He spoke about the people dragging the stone up to be carved. Then, they had skilled people shaping the stones ready to be used to build the pyramid, then other people would drag the stones to the pyramid, and once there, another team of workers would put the stones into place.

Milton thought about what a lot of hard work all this was. He asked: why do all this hard work to build a pyramid? The caretaker explained that the Egyptians believed that Pharaohs - the rulers of the land - were gods walking the Earth, and when they died they needed to return safely to the heavens, so they built pyramids to help them transport back to the afterlife. The pyramids were aligned with the sun, moon and stars, so that they could find their way safely into the next life.

The caretaker took Milton to a smaller pyramid which was already fully built but not yet used. They walked inside the pyramid to see painters painting on the walls of the pyramid. The caretaker explained that the painters paint the stories of the pharaoh's life on the walls, and the stories of the pharaoh's journey into the next life, too.

He explained that the Pharaoh gets placed inside the pyramid with their most prized possessions to take with them into the afterlife. They then get sealed in the pyramid so that no-one can disturb them. There are traps and secret passages hidden in the pyramid, to try to stop people finding their way to the Pharaoh's personal chamber. This gives the Pharaoh time to get to the afterlife in peace.

Milton watched as a priest appeared at the recently-built pyramid and walked just inside the entrance. He wondered why a new pyramid was being built when this one was just being finished. The caretaker explained that the pyramids took many years to make, so they started building the pyramid when the Pharaoh came into power. The new pyramid was being built for the new Pharaoh; the pyramid just being finished was for the previous Pharaoh.

The priest raised his staff in the air. The staff had a perfectly smooth, polished crystal on the handle end. He said what sounded like a magical chant. Milton saw blue sparks, like lightning, erupt from the staff, zigzagging through the air, and striking different places on the walls and ceiling inside. There was a loud crack like thunder as the sparks jumped from the staff, and popping zapping sounds as the sparks jumped around the walls.

Milton wondered what was happening. The caretaker explained that the priest was finishing the rituals for preparing the pyramid for the Pharaoh. He had to ward off anything bad, and leave this as a good place for the Pharaoh to make his journey to the afterlife.

After a whole day of exploring the pyramids and the different work everyone was doing, and seeing how well everyone seemed to be working as a team to get such big and difficult structures made, he felt himself drifting away from Egypt. He saw the caretaker walk away and vanish, he walked back to his school desk which had appeared, then he noticed Egypt disappearing, as sand turned back to autumn leaves. The wheel turned back into the roundabout, and he could see the window to the classroom appearing between him and his view of the autumn scene outside. He could hear the teacher talking in the background about Egypt.

He gradually paid the teacher more attention as he drifted back from his day-dream, back to the real world in school, just as you can drift back and slowly open your eyes, when you feel ready, as *you continue to feel relaxed.*

Printed in Great Britain
by Amazon